PORPOISES

Printed in Hong Kong

99 00 01 02 03 5 4 3 2 1

Library of Congress Cataloging-in-Publication Data
Read, Andrew J.
Porpoises / Andrew Read.
p. cm. — (World life library)
ISBN 0-89658-420-8
1. Porpoises. I. Title. II. Series.
QL737.C424R435 1999   98-51770
599.53'9–dc21   CIP

Distributed in Canada by Raincoast Books, 8680 Cambie Street, Vancouver, B.C. V6P 6M9

Published by Voyageur Press, Inc.
123 North Second Street, P. O. Box 338, Stillwater, MN 55082, U.S.A.
651-430-2210, fax 651-430-2211

Educators, fundraisers, premium and gift buyers, publicists and marketing managers: Looking for creative products and new sales ideas? Voyageur Press books are available at special discounts when purchased in quantities, and special editions can be created to your specifications. For details contact the marketing department at 800-888-9653.

PORPOISES

Andrew Read

WORLDLIFE
LIBRARY

Voyageur Press

Contents

Introduction

It is a typical summer morning in the Bay of Fundy, Canada. The fog forms a wet, gray blanket as we motor along the rocky shoreline in our small boat. Slowly, a structure looms out of the mist. It is a herring weir, a large heart-shaped trap made of wooden stakes and netting designed to catch fish that swim close to shore. We turn off our motor and tie up to one of the stakes. After a minute or so, the quiet is broken by a puffing sound as a harbor porpoise surfaces inside the weir. Just as quickly, the porpoise disappears, leaving a circle of ripples on the water's glassy surface. The porpoise has followed a school of herring – its favorite prey – into the weir and is now trapped inside.

We sit and watch the porpoise until we hear the sound of an approaching boat. The boat carries six fishermen and a large, fine-meshed seine net (which is used to remove herring from the weir). It is soon joined by a second, larger boat that will carry the herring to the cannery. The quiet is shattered by the sounds of diesel engines, hydraulic winches and fishermen shouting instructions inside the weir. The porpoise starts to swim faster, surfacing with a splash, trying to stay away from the boats. The fishermen tie one end of the net to a weir stake and slowly drop it around the inside of the weir, banging the hull with an oar to keep the herring away from the boat. Eventually the seine boat completes its journey around the inner perimeter of the weir, and the fishermen tie both ends of the net together. The bottom of the net is drawn together by a line that runs through a series of rings, and now forms a large bag containing the herring and porpoise. The herring swim in a massive, dense silvery school which occasionally parts as the porpoise darts through. The net is slowly drawn closer together forming a smaller and smaller space

A harbor porpoise surfaces in the Bay of Fundy.

within which the herring and porpoise can swim. Herring gulls swarm around the weir, picking up any fish that strays too close to the surface.

The porpoise is now charging through the water, looking for an opening in the seine net through which it might make an escape. Suddenly, it veers towards the net and becomes tangled in folds of the fine mesh. As it struggles to free itself, bubbles of air escape from its blowhole. The porpoise is trapped and cannot reach the surface to breathe. Without help, the animal will die in a few minutes. Scenes like this are repeated thousands of times each year around the world, as porpoises become entangled and die in fishing nets.

Fortunately, this porpoise will be one of the lucky few to survive such an encounter. With the fishermen's help, we have placed Rob, our diver, inside the weir to deal with just such a situation. Rob swims down to the entangled porpoise, and after a few tense moments frees it from the net and carries it back up to the surface where it can breathe. Holding the porpoise in his arms, he swims across the weir to our boat, where we lift the animal out of the water and place it gently on a foam mat. We keep the porpoise's skin moist by sponging it with sea water as we move back out of the weir and into the fog-shrouded bay. The porpoise is calm, but moves its head from side to side, inspecting its strange new environment.

Once we are well away from the weir, we stop the boat and conduct a quick examination as the porpoise lies quietly on the mat. We gently roll the porpoise over on its side and determine that it is a male. From his size, just over 3 ft (1 m) long, we estimate that the porpoise is a little over a year old; it has been away from its mother for only a month or two. We obtain a small sample of blood to evaluate his health and clip a small, numbered plastic tag on his dorsal fin. Our examination is brief and, in less than ten minutes, we are ready to release him back into the sea. We gently lower the porpoise over the side of the boat and support him as he scans the water below him. After a breath, and with a quick beat of his flukes, he dives away from the boat. A few moments

Harbor porpoises are stocky animals with small dorsal fins and flippers.
Their robust shape and small appendages help to keep these small marine mammals
warm in a cold environment. Unlike dolphins, porpoises lack a prominent beak or rostrum.

Seining a herring weir in the Bay of Fundy.

later, he surfaces several feet from the boat and then disappears into the fog.

This story is typical of many porpoises that we release from herring weirs each summer in the Bay of Fundy. The success of this program is due to the unusual nature of the fishery, which allows porpoises to survive while trapped in a weir, the hard work and cooperation of weir fishermen, and financial support from conservation organizations. Unfortunately, most entanglements in other types of fishing gear end with the death of the porpoise. Sadly, there has been little progress in reducing the number of porpoises killed in this way

Biologist Andrew Westgate releases a harbor porpoise outside a herring weir.

and little public outcry about such wasteful fishing practices.

Perhaps the reason there has been so little public concern about the conservation problems faced by porpoises is due to a lack of familiarity with these animals. They are not maintained frequently in oceanaria or featured on television and few people have ever seen one in the wild. Most species of porpoises are shy, retiring animals, uncomfortable in the presence of humans. This book introduces these enigmatic animals and highlights some of the pressing conservation problems they face.

Porpoises and Dolphins

What are porpoises and how are they different from dolphins? In the past, and still in some places today, the common names 'porpoise' and 'dolphin' have been used interchangeably. In many parts of the United States, for example, fishermen refer to dolphins as porpoises, to distinguish the mammals from the dolphin fish, also known as mahi-mahi or dorado. Unfortunately, some scientists have followed this convention, further contributing to the confusion.

Fortunately, there is a scientific classification system that helps to sort out problems introduced by shared common names. In this classification system, known as taxonomy, scientists arrange species in groups according to their evolutionary history. Because porpoises and dolphins share a long common evolutionary ancestry, both are placed in the order Cetacea, the group of mammals that also includes the great whales. All cetaceans are completely aquatic and show common features, such as a streamlined shape, a lack of external hind limbs, a propulsive tail fluke, and blowholes.

Porpoises and dolphins are also classified together as odontocetes, or toothed whales. The odontocetes also include the larger toothed whales, such as the sperm whale. Not surprisingly, all toothed whales possess teeth, separating them from the great whales that filter their food from the water with plates of baleen. Another common feature of odontocetes (at least in all dolphins and porpoises studied to date) is the ability to echolocate, or to use sound to detect objects in the environment. Porpoises and dolphins are separated taxonomically into two different families, porpoises in the family Phocoenidae and dolphins in the family Delphinidae. These two family names are derived from the Latin names for porpoise and dolphin, respectively. In this

Like all toothed whales, harbor porpoises have a single blowhole.

classification scheme, separated at the family level, dolphins and porpoises are considered to be as different as dogs and cats.

The biological differences between porpoises and dolphins are quite striking. First, porpoises and dolphins have very different appearances. In comparison to many dolphins, porpoises are small, seldom exceeding 6 ft 6 in (2 m) in length. Porpoises tend to be more robust than dolphins and their dorsal fins are usually smaller and more triangular. The facial features of animals in the two groups are also very different. Unlike most dolphins, porpoises lack a prominent rostrum or beak. Finally, porpoise teeth are spade-shaped while those of dolphins are usually conical.

Many aspects of the behavior of porpoises and dolphins are also very different. With some notable exceptions, porpoises are shy animals that do not approach boats or exhibit the characteristic exuberance of dolphins at the water's surface. In most cases, all we see of a porpoise is a small dorsal fin as the animal surfaces to breathe. Their shy disposition has been known for centuries. In his *Encyclopedia of Natural History*, the Roman author Pliny the Elder commented that porpoises possess 'a certain gloomy air, as they lack the sportive nature of the dolphin'. This is more likely a reflection of our limitations as terrestrial observers than of the nature of the porpoises themselves. Like dolphins, porpoises have a rich social life and complex patterns of behavior, but most of their lives are spent far from the surface, where we cannot see them.

These differences between dolphins and porpoises are overshadowed by their similarities. In addition to their common ancestry as toothed whales, as noted above, many aspects of the biology of porpoises and dolphins are very similar. In evolutionary terms, both groups have successfully mastered life in an aquatic medium that presents a daunting set of challenges to any mammal. In the next few chapters, I will introduce the diversity of porpoises and describe some of their adaptations to life in the sea.

A harbor porpoise rolls lazily at the surface on a calm day.
Tiny bumps, or tubercles, are present on the leading edge of the dorsal fin.
These tubercles are present in several species of porpoises, but their function is unknown.

Diversity

There are six species of true porpoises in the family Phocoenidae. By far the best known species is the harbor porpoise, which has been studied since the time of Aristotle. Much less is known about the other five species and one, the vaquita, was first described by scientists in 1958. All porpoises share characteristics of appearance, ecology and behavior that distinguish them from other toothed whales.

The harbor porpoise (*Phocoena phocoena*) is found in coastal waters of the North Atlantic, North Pacific and Black Sea. In the United Kingdom, this species is usually known as the common porpoise, or simply as the porpoise. In other parts of the world, harbor porpoises are sometimes called 'puffers' or 'tumblers', referring to the sound and motion of their surfacing patterns. These porpoises prefer the cold, productive waters of the continental shelf, where food is abundant. Like all porpoises, harbor porpoises are small animals, usually less than 6 ft 6 in (2 m) in length and seldom exceeding 165 lb (75 kg) in weight. They are very attractive animals, with dark gray backs, mottled gray flanks and a white belly. One or more dark stripes extends from the flipper to the angle of the mouth. The pattern of coloration is complex and unique to each individual. Their body shape is stocky which, together with their small fins and dorsal fin, helps minimize heat loss to a cold environment. The dorsal fin is triangular and, like those of other porpoises, has several rows of tiny bumps or tubercles along its leading edge. We do not know what function these tubercles might serve.

The Burmeister's porpoise (*Phocoena spinipinnis*) is found only around the coasts of South America. On the Pacific coast, the species ranges from northern Peru, south to Tierra del Fuego and on the Atlantic coast as far north

Dall's porpoises possess a striking pattern of black and white pigmentation.

as southern Brazil. Named after the biologist who described the species in 1865, Burmeister's porpoises are about the same size as harbor porpoises. This species is much darker than the harbor porpoise, with a lead-gray back and sides and a lighter gray belly. Like the harbor porpoise, the face of the Burmeister's porpoise has a complex pattern of coloration, with subtle eye and lip patches and stripes extending from the flippers to the mouth. The dorsal fin of the Burmeister's porpoise is unusual in both its shape and placement. The fin is small, extends at a low angle and is placed so far back that it looks as if it is sliding off the animal. There are several rows of tubercles on the dorsal fin, which give this species its Latin scientific name, *Phocoena spinipinnis*, or spiny-finned porpoise. The species is referred to as the *marsopa espinosa* (spiny porpoise) or, more frequently, 'tonino', throughout Latin America.

The smallest porpoise is the vaquita (*Phocoena sinus*), a close relative of both the harbor and Burmeister's porpoise. This species is found only in a tiny area of the Upper Gulf of California, Mexico, also known as the Sea of Cortez. Although it is found closer to the harbor porpoise in California than the Burmeister's porpoise in Peru, genetic evidence indicates that the vaquita is more closely related to the latter. It is likely that vaquitas colonized the Gulf of California during a period when the earth's climate was considerably colder than today, allowing ancestors of Burmeister's porpoises to slip across the equator and into the Gulf of California. Scientists were not aware of the existence of this species until 1958, when Ken Norris and Bill McFarland described a weathered skull that they found on a Mexican beach. Even today, only a handful of biologists have seen the species alive.

Sadly, the vaquita is the most endangered whale, dolphin or porpoise in the world's oceans. Large numbers of individuals have been killed in fishing nets and now only a few hundred remain in the Gulf of California. Vaquitas are beautiful animals, with dark eye rings and flipper stripes, a tall dorsal fin and large, pointed flippers. Their large appendages – in contrast to the small fins

There are two color forms of Dall's porpoise – the more common dalli type shown here
and the truei type, in which the white pigmentation extends much further forward on the body.
The dorsal fin of mature male Dall's porpoises is canted further forward than the dorsal fin of females.

*Finless porpoises are quite dark at birth, but rapidly acquire the
light gray coloration that is typical of older animals. As their name indicates, finless
porpoises lack a dorsal fin, although they possess the tubercles found on dorsal fins of other
porpoise species. Finless porpoises are restricted to the warm coastal waters of southeast Asia.*

and flippers of the harbor porpoise – may act as radiators, allowing vaquitas to dissipate excess heat in warm water.

Finless porpoises (*Neophocaena phocaenoides*) are found in the rivers and shallow coastal waters of southeast Asia, as far north as Japan and as far west as the Persian Gulf. The species was first described by the French naturalist Georges Cuvier in 1829. This is the only species of porpoise to inhabit fresh water on a regular basis and one population is found only in the fresh waters of the Yangtze River in China. The most striking feature of the finless porpoise is its lack of a dorsal fin, although several rows of tubercles are present along the back. The flippers are very long and bluntly pointed. Unlike other porpoises, the finless porpoise is uniformly gray in color. In many ways, the finless porpoise resembles a small, gray beluga whale.

A rare photograph of a spectacled porpoise in the wild.

Unlike the preceding four species, Dall's porpoises (*Phocoenoides dalli*) are found frequently in the open ocean. They occur across the northern Pacific Ocean from California to Japan and as far north as the Pribilof Islands. The species is named after the naturalist William Dall who described the first specimen in 1873. Dall's porpoises are very stocky animals, with a head that appears small relative to their muscular body. They have a dramatic pattern of coloration. The body is black, except for a large white patch on the abdomen that extends to the belly. There are two color forms of this species that are distinguished by the extent and position of this white patch. The trailing edges of the dorsal fin and flukes are fringed with white or light gray. The dorsal fin of adult males is canted forwards, allowing researchers to identify mature male Dall's porpoises in the field.

Spectacled porpoises (*Australophocoena dioptrica*) are the most poorly known species in the family, primarily because of their habitat in the remote and frigid waters of the sub-Antarctic. The first sighting of this species was recorded by one of Captain James Cook's expeditions in January 1775, but an intact specimen was not examined until 1912. Since that time, almost all information has come from stranded animals. Most of these observations have been made by a single biologist, Natalie Goodall, who works on the windswept beaches of Tierra del Fuego, at the southernmost tip of South America. From Natalie's specimens and a handful of others found on the beaches of remote islands, we believe that this species is found in offshore waters around the Antarctic continent. Like Dall's porpoises, spectacled porpoises have a striking pattern of coloration. The upper half of the body is jet black and is separated clearly from the white lower half. The dorsal fin and upper flukes are black and the flippers may be white, gray or black. The species owes its name to the presence of a dark patch, outlined by a thin white line, that encircles the eye. Spectacled porpoises also have dark lips that contrast with the white of the lower face.

The evolutionary relationships among these six species of porpoises have not yet been completely resolved and taxonomists continue to debate the most appropriate way of grouping the species. The recent discovery of a hybrid between a Dall's porpoise and a harbor porpoise, for example, has led some biologists to question whether these two species should be separated at the genus level. Clearly there is much still to learn about the taxonomy and evolutionary history of porpoises.

Harbor porpoises are found in the coastal temperate waters of the northern hemisphere.

Life History

We know a considerable amount about the reproductive biology of harbor and Dall's porpoises, because biologists have examined thousands of individuals that were killed in fisheries or taken by hunters. Our knowledge of reproduction in the other species is rather scant. In both harbor and Dall's porpoises, pregnancy lasts for about 11 months. Most births occur in the spring and early summer, so females can nurse their calves when food is most available. By the time winter arrives, calves are feeding on their own and they place less nutritional demand on their mothers.

Compared to those of larger cetaceans, porpoise calves are tiny. At birth, harbor porpoise calves are only 27½ in (70 cm) long and weigh about 11 lb (5 kg). The calves are delivered tail-first from the warmth of their mother's womb into a cold and unforgiving environment. They must immediately surface, breathe and learn to keep up with their mothers. At sea, it is easy to identify newborn porpoises by their small size, floppy dorsal fins and fetal folds, or 'tiger stripes', on their sides. The stripes are a result of being folded over in their mother's uterus during pregnancy. The calves start nursing immediately, as they are born with little blubber and need their mothers' rich milk to fatten up and stay warm. Young calves are awkward swimmers, and bob to the surface to breathe, rather than rolling gracefully like older animals.

Female Dall's and harbor porpoises often become pregnant each year. In the Bay of Fundy, female harbor porpoises give birth in May and then five or six weeks later, ovulate, mate and become pregnant again. At this point the females are simultaneously pregnant and nursing their new calves. Fortunately, the energetic demands of the fetus are quite low during early pregnancy, when the mother is producing a large quantity of milk for her young calf. Conversely,

Most harbor porpoises are found alone or in groups of two or three individuals.

when the fetus is growing rapidly during the last trimester of pregnancy, the older calf is taking solid food and is no longer completely dependent on its mother for milk. Nevertheless, this is a very demanding schedule for the mother, who requires an abundant supply of food to satisfy her needs as well as those of her calf and growing fetus. With these additional demands, it is not surprising that adult female porpoises eat more than other porpoises.

Calves are born without teeth and, for the first few months of life, are completely dependent on their mothers' milk. Their teeth erupt when they are a few months old and the young porpoises begin to take solid food, as they learn to catch small fish and other prey, probably as they accompany their mothers on foraging excursions. As most females reproduce each year, the older offspring must be weaned upon the arrival of the new calf. After the calves are weaned, they have a few years of independence before they begin to reproduce. Compared to other toothed whales, this juvenile period is very brief. For example, harbor porpoises usually reach sexual maturity in their second, third or fourth year of life; at this age, young bottlenose dolphins are still with their mothers. During this juvenile period, harbor porpoises grow rapidly, reaching their full adult size shortly after they become sexually mature.

One of the defining characteristics of porpoises is their small size, at least relative to other cetaceans. The evolutionary ancestors of modern porpoises were larger animals, about the size of bottlenose dolphins. The reasons for this evolutionary trend are unclear, but the consequences of being small are quite profound. Most importantly, small porpoises tend to lose body heat to their environment at a rapid rate. Scientists have debated how porpoises manage to stay warm in a cold, conductive environment for many years. It now appears that porpoises maintain their body temperature with a thick layer of insulative blubber, a sophisticated series of counter-current heat exchangers in

Dall's porpoises at the surface near the coast of Alaska.

their extremities, and by minimizing the surface area over which heat can be lost. These adaptations allow porpoises to thrive in cold waters that would quickly incapacitate and kill a human being.

The porpoise in the foreground is logging.

Their intensive reproductive schedule takes its toll and porpoises have a relatively short life expectancy. Biologists estimate the ages of porpoises by counting layers in the dentine of their teeth, much like rings in a tree trunk. Most harbor porpoises do not live past their mid teens, although a few specimens in their early twenties have been found. Almost all samples examined by biologists have come from populations of porpoises heavily impacted by fisheries or hunting, in which the life expectancy of individuals may be reduced. We do not know what the typical life span of a porpoise might be in a population not affected by human activities. This relatively short life span provides another contrast between the biology of porpoises and dolphins. The maximum longevity of many dolphin species is much greater, with some bottlenose dolphins living for 50 years or more.

Until now, most information on the life history of porpoises has come from studies of dead animals. As noted in the following chapters, it is difficult to identify individual porpoises at sea and follow their lives to document patterns of births and deaths, as we do for many other mammals. Biologists face considerable challenges in overcoming these difficulties to increase our knowledge of these animals.

*Harbor porpoises are one of the most frequently stranded
cetaceans in Europe and North America. Unlike some other species of toothed whales,
porpoises usually strand alone and not in large groups. Researchers have been able to learn a
considerable amount about the natural history of this species from examining these stranded porpoises.*

Ecology

Porpoises seldom bring their prey to the surface where we can see it, so we must rely on indirect methods to determine what they eat. Most of what we know about their diet comes from studies of porpoises killed by hunters or in fishing nets; we can piece together information by identifying the remains of prey items in their stomachs. Like all cetaceans, porpoises have a three-chambered stomach that allows them to consume a large number of prey in each meal. Biologists have examined many harbor and Dall's porpoise stomachs, and a few from Burmeister's and finless porpoises. In contrast, we know very little about the food of the vaquita and spectacled porpoise. All porpoises feed on small, individual prey items that are usually less than 12 in (30 cm) in length. Porpoise teeth are not very useful for chewing or tearing, but are well suited for grasping individual prey. Once captured, porpoises turn their prey head-first and swallow it whole, so that fish spines do not become stuck in their throats.

The diets of harbor and Dall's porpoises reflect their habitats. Harbor porpoises live in shallow, coastal waters and feed on small fish near the sea floor. Their diet is dominated by fatty species such as herring, capelin and sprat that are rich in energy. In contrast, Dall's porpoises live in the open ocean and feed on small fish, squid and crustaceans in the water column. Much of their prey is found in the deep-scattering layer, an aggregation of small animals that migrate towards the surface each night and return to the depths during the day.

In Peru, Burmeister's porpoises feed mainly on anchoveta. This small, silvery fish occurs in vast schools and is the most important prey of many marine mammals and seabirds in the coastal Humboldt current. At irregular intervals this productive ecosystem is disrupted by the *El Niño*-Southern

Porpoises spend most of their lives out of the view of human observers.

Ocean phenomenon. During particularly severe *El Niño* events, as seen in 1997, the anchoveta either die or leave these waters. Anchoveta predators, such as the Burmeister's porpoise, must find an alternative food source or starve. From the emaciated bodies of Burmeister's porpoises stranded on Peruvian beaches during the most recent *El Niño*, it appears that many animals starve to death during these events. Many other marine mammals, including fur seals and sea lions, suffer the same fate, indicating the critical importance of anchoveta to this ecosystem.

The effects of *El Niño* on Burmeister's porpoises are extreme, but all porpoises face the problem of finding enough food to eat in a constantly varying environment. Unlike large whales that can fast for months, porpoises are too small to store enough energy to survive for long without food. Porpoises store most of their energy reserves as lipids in the blubber, which also serves several other important functions, such as insulation, streamlining, and providing buoyancy. So, if a porpoise cannot find food and uses the lipids in its blubber to obtain energy, it may compromise the other functions of this important tissue. Physiologist Heather Koopman has found that, in times of food shortages, porpoises initially obtain energy by metabolizing blubber lipids. They only use the inner layer of blubber, however, and even a starving porpoise will retain a $1/3$-in- (1-cm-) thick blubber layer to stay warm. At this point, the porpoise must turn to other sources of energy, such as protein in muscle, to survive. In addition to the need for energy, dehydration also becomes a problem. Without any source of fresh water, porpoises must obtain all of their metabolic water from food. A harbor porpoise cannot survive without food for much more than a week before it encounters serious physiological problems. Eventually, a starving porpoise is so weakened that it cannot swim and either strands on a beach or dies at sea. Each spring, we find the emaciated bodies of young, recently weaned porpoises that died of starvation along the eastern shores of the United States.

A Burmeister's porpoise at the fish market in Pucusana, Peru. For many years Peruvian fishermen captured and sold porpoises and dolphins for their meat. Thanks to the concerted efforts of concerned biologists and recent protective legislation, this practice is now outlawed in Peru.

A herring weir in the Bay of Fundy, Canada. These large
traps are designed to capture herring that swim along shore at night. The herring
encounter the leader that extends from the trap to the shore and swim into the mouth of the
heart-shaped weir. Herring predators, such as harbor porpoises, often follow their prey into the weirs.

A few of these stranded porpoises are fortunate enough to be found alive and taken to an aquarium. More and more facilities are becoming successful at treating stranded harbor porpoises, eventually rehabilitating and releasing them back into the wild. The most successful program of this kind is run by Ron Kastelein at the Harderwijk Marine Mammal Park in the Netherlands. Ron and his staff have successfully nursed many emaciated and sick porpoises back to health. This has provided a unique opportunity to study the porpoises before they are released.

The amount of food required by a porpoise depends on its size, activity level, reproductive state, and the quality of the food itself. As already noted, adult female porpoises must eat more than other porpoises to provide the additional energy needed during lactation and pregnancy. Working with captive animals, researchers in Japan and the Netherlands have tried to determine exactly how much food is needed for a porpoise to maintain its body weight. These studies indicate that young harbor porpoises need to consume 7-8 per cent of their body weight per day. Thus, a young, growing porpoise might need to consume 20 or 30 herring a day to meet its energy requirements. The amount actually consumed by wild porpoises will vary considerably due to the factors noted above.

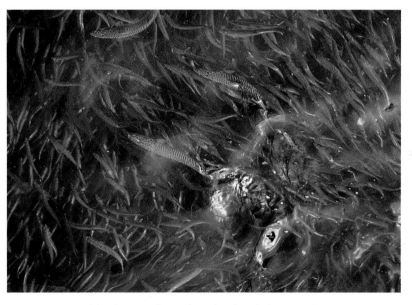

Herring and mackerel schools in a weir.

We know quite a lot about what porpoises eat, but very little about how they find and catch their food. To better understand how porpoises find their prey, my colleague Andrew Westgate developed an ingenious electronic tag to study the diving behavior of harbor porpoises. The tag contains a small radio transmitter and a data logger that measures depth at intervals and records this information on a microchip. Once the tag is retrieved, the data can be downloaded to a personal computer. Such data loggers are used routinely with seals and sea lions who haul out on shore, where researchers can apply and remove the tags quite freely. We were able to attach Andrew's tags to the porpoises released from herring weirs in the Bay of Fundy, but we had no way to recapture the animals to get the tags back (not surprisingly, porpoises seldom swim back into a weir after being released). Instead of trying to recapture the porpoises, Andrew designed the tags so that they would automatically release from the porpoise after a pre-set period and float to the surface. The small VHF radio in the tag allowed us to follow the porpoise at sea and to recover the package once it was jettisoned. We equipped nine harbor porpoises with these tags and managed to retrieve eight of them. The ninth was found by a fisherman on a beach in Nova Scotia, 18 months after it was deployed, with the data still intact.

From the data recorded by the tags, we discovered that harbor porpoises are quite remarkable divers. The tagged porpoises made dives of up to five minutes in duration. The deepest dive was made by an adult female who reached 735 ft (224 m), the deepest part of the Bay of Fundy. The porpoises dove rapidly, spent a minute or two near the bottom, and then returned quickly to the surface. We think that these dives were feeding trips, in which porpoises dove to the sea floor to look for prey. The data in the tags held as many questions as answers for us and we are still working to understand how porpoises actually find and catch prey during these dives. It seems unlikely that a porpoise resting at the surface can detect a school of herring 330 ft (100 m) below it, so how does an animal search for prey while conserving oxygen on each dive?

Researchers use small electronic tags, affixed to the dorsal fins of porpoises, to follow the movements and behavior of these animals. These tags can be used to monitor the health of individuals after release from herring weirs and provide unique insights into the behavior of porpoises in the wild.

Due to their relatively small size, porpoises are preyed on by killer whales and several species of large sharks. Here a killer whale tosses a Dall's porpoise into the air along the Pacific coast of North America. Killer whales are frequent predators of many marine mammals in this region.

Their small size makes porpoises vulnerable to predation by large sharks and killer whales. In the Bay of Fundy, white sharks are the most frequent predators of harbor porpoises. Some of the biggest white sharks in the world have been reported here, including some large specimens from herring weirs. From the remains of harbor porpoises in the stomachs of white sharks, it seems that attacks come most frequently from behind and below the porpoise. The shark severs the tail stock of a porpoise and then swallows both halves. We have seen very few porpoises bearing the scars of past encounters with sharks, and it is likely that most attacks are fatal. Along the northwest coast of North America, killer whales are important predators of both harbor porpoises and Dall's porpoises.

In some other areas of the world porpoises face a threat from another, unexpected source. In Scotland, researchers Harry Ross, Ben Wilson and their colleagues noticed a large number of stranded harbor porpoises with evidence of severe trauma, including extensive bruising, broken bones and ruptured organs. It wasn't clear what was responsible, although the wounds were not consistent with any type of human activity. Many of the stranded porpoises had short, parallel cuts in their skin that looked as if they might have been made by some animal's teeth. By matching these wounds with the jaws of bottlenose dolphins from museums, the researchers were able to identify the unlikely culprit. Subsequent video footage confirmed that, in the Moray Firth, bottlenose dolphins attack and kill harbor porpoises. At first, the reason for these attacks was not apparent. The dolphins did not eat the porpoises and it is very rare for one mammal to kill another if predation is not involved.

Further work by the Scottish researchers showed that bottlenose dolphins in their area also practice infanticide: killing calves of their own species. A young bottlenose dolphin calf is almost exactly the same size as a harbor porpoise and the Scottish researchers suggest that the dolphins may be practicing their dark skills on the porpoises.

Behavior

Most porpoises are shy and do not approach boats or seek contact with humans. An exception to this general rule is the Dall's porpoise which enjoys riding the bow and stern wakes of boats. Studying porpoise behavior is challenging: I have spent many frustrating hours in kayaks and small boats trying to follow harbor porpoises. Even when tracking a tagged porpoise, it is hard to keep the animal in sight for long. It is also very difficult to tell individual porpoises apart at sea. Many dolphins carry natural markings, such as notches on their dorsal fins, that researchers can use to identify individuals. Few porpoises carry these markings and, to most observers, one porpoise looks much like another. Finally, we seldom see more than the back of an animal as it surfaces and then disappears from view. In contrast, dolphins ride the bows of boats, leap, chase, bite and roll over each other and slap their flukes on the water's surface. This has led some observers to suggest that porpoise social behavior is limited. However when researchers have managed to overcome the obstacles studying porpoise behavior, we find that their lives are as rich and complex as those of their larger relatives.

As in most mammals, the strongest social bond is between a mother and her calf. A newborn calf stays close to its mother, usually positioned on one side just behind the dorsal fin. This enables the pair to stay in physical contact and allows the calf to draft along in its mother's wake, reducing the amount of energy it must expend swimming. As the calf grows and begins to feed for itself, it spends more time away from its mother. The female may leave the calf at the surface when she makes deep feeding dives. Females with calves are often found together, perhaps because they must feed more intensively than other porpoises while also protecting their offspring from predators.

Dall's porpoises often produce a 'rooster tail' when they surface.

The arrival of a new sibling may not be a welcome event in the life of the older calf. In Sognefjord, Norway, I watched a female harbor porpoise with a calf only a few hours old. They were approached by a third, small animal, likely the female's previous calf. As the older calf approached, the female lashed out and struck it with her flukes, driving it away. We do not know whether older calves continue to associate with their mothers after the birth of a new calf, but groups of three porpoises, including a mother, calf and third small animal, are a common sight in the late spring and early summer. Occasionally we see young calves being tossed into the air, perhaps by their older siblings.

On calm days, female harbor porpoises may rest motionless at the surface while their calves nurse. Other porpoises also engage in this behavior, known as 'logging'. Some logging porpoises are simply resting, but others gradually turn on their axis as they scan the water below. A porpoise's usual surfacing motion is a gentle rolling arc, but when excited or in heavy seas, they will charge through the water, creating a large splash. Dall's porpoises are faster swimmers than the other species and routinely produce a 'rooster tail' of spray when they surface.

Porpoises are generally seen alone or in groups containing a few individuals. These are not stable associations, but ephemeral groupings that change as individuals join or leave. In fact, it is often difficult to decide exactly what constitutes a group of porpoises. On sunny, calm days in the Bay of Fundy, small groups of porpoises may be dispersed over areas of several hectares. Suddenly, some of the groups will coalesce into a tight aggregation, rocket through a narrow pass and then spread out again to feed on the other side. The porpoises act in a co-ordinated fashion, even though they are separated by hundreds of feet. It is likely that animals are in acoustic contact during these episodes, even though they seem to be behaving independently.

Porpoises seldom form large schools, such as those found in dolphins of

Very little is known of the social behavior of Dall's porpoises.

Dall's and harbor porpoises are found together in several areas
of the Pacific and hybrids between the two species have been reported.
Anomalously colored Dall's porpoises, such as this gray animal in Haro Strait,
British Columbia, may represent additional cases of hybridism between the two species.

the open ocean. Occasionally, tens or hundreds of feeding porpoises are observed together, but these are rare events and the aggregations soon disperse. This tendency to occur alone or in small groups is reflected in stranding records. Porpoises tend to strand alone, not *en masse* like some of the larger toothed whales, such as pilot and sperm whales.

It is possible to follow the movements of porpoises for brief periods at sea, but it is not practical to do this for long periods. To study the movements of individual porpoises over periods of months, Andrew Westgate and I teamed up again to use small electronic tags that transmit data to orbiting satellites. In this way, we are able to track porpoise movements from our offices. We have used these transmitters on 16 harbor porpoises released from herring weirs in the Bay of Fundy. We have received data from some of these porpoises for more than six months and are continually amazed by their movements. Porpoises from the Bay of Fundy have moved throughout the Gulf of Maine and as far south as Nantucket Island, south of Cape Cod, a distance of over 250 nautical miles (460 km).

The tagged porpoises typically make rapid movements between areas, where they stay for days or weeks. Many of these areas contain dense schools of herring and porpoises seem to move from one area of herring concentration to another. These tags have also shown us that individual porpoises do not form stable associations, apart from mothers and calves. For example, we tagged three large adult males, Aramis, Porthos and Athos, on the same day and in the same herring weir. The trio immediately split up and spent the summer, autumn and early winter in different areas of the Bay of Fundy and Gulf of Maine, never meeting again. This amazing technology has given us insight that we could not have obtained in any other way. Now when I walk into my office in North Carolina on a blustery January morning, I can switch on my computer and locate a porpoise that we tagged months ago in the Bay of Fundy.

Most of our knowledge about reproductive behavior has come from observations of captive porpoises or has been inferred from dead animals. In captivity, porpoises exhibit frequent sexual behavior and, as is the case with dolphins, sex seems to be a regular part of their social life in addition to serving a reproductive function. From dead specimens, we know that male harbor porpoises possess testes that are very large for their body size, reaching 4 per cent of total body weight during the breeding season. Mature males show very little evidence of aggressive interactions with each other, such as scarring or broken teeth. In addition, male harbor porpoises are smaller than females, an unusual feature among mammals. These characteristics suggests that male harbor porpoises may compete with each other not by fighting, but by producing large quantities of sperm and mating with as many females as possible in an attempt to displace each other's sperm. These ideas are still only hypotheses and need to be tested by observations of wild porpoises during the breeding season. The mating systems of other porpoise species are unknown.

Another poorly known aspect of porpoise biology is their acoustic behavior. We know a fair amount about the kinds of sounds produced by harbor porpoises and a little about their hearing capabilities, but virtually nothing about how they use sound in their daily lives. Porpoises produce sound over a wide range of frequencies, although most of their sounds are well above the upper limits of human hearing. Many of these sounds are clicks used in echolocation to detect, locate and identify objects in a porpoise's environment. Captive porpoises are skilled at using echolocation to detect and discriminate between objects — even those buried in sand — but we do not know how porpoises use echolocation to navigate or find prey in the wild. Porpoises do not appear to produce the whistles used in dolphin communication and how they use sound to communicate is completely unknown.

Conservation

Most species of porpoises are threatened to some extent by human activities. The species in most immediate danger is the highly endangered vaquita, but there is also reason for concern about populations of harbor, finless, Burmeister's and Dall's porpoises. In several cases, porpoises have disappeared entirely from areas where they were once common. The harbor porpoise, for example, is now rare or absent from the English Channel and the Baltic Sea. Only the spectacled porpoise, in the remote waters of the Southern Ocean, is largely unaffected by human activities.

The greatest threat to most porpoises is accidental death in fishing nets, sometimes referred to as 'by-catch' or 'incidental take'. This occurs when porpoises become entangled in fishing gear and cannot reach the surface to breath. Like other cetaceans, porpoises are voluntary breathers and, unlike humans, do not breathe when unconscious. Thus, once an entangled porpoise loses consciousness, it will die from asphyxiation.

Although porpoises are killed in many types of fishing gear, most accidental deaths occur in gill nets. These nets are typically several feet deep and can extend for hundreds or thousands of feet in length. Gill nets are transparent underwater and are designed to entangle fish around the gills as they attempt to swim through the net. The size of the net mesh reflects the size of the fish that the net is designed to catch: small mesh nets catch small fish and larger mesh nets catch larger fish. Unfortunately, porpoises are about the same size as the larger fish that the nets are intended to catch. The nets can be anchored on the sea floor to catch bottom-dwelling species such as cod, or left to drift at the surface to catch top-water species, such as salmon. In either configuration, they catch porpoises.

We do not understand why, with such a sophisticated echolocation system, porpoises are prone to becoming entangled in gill nets and other fishing gear. An echolocating porpoise should be able to detect and avoid nets, but many do not. It is possible that porpoises detect the nets, but do not perceive them as dangerous. Alternatively, porpoises may not detect the nets simply because they are not constantly echolocating. Finally, porpoises may be echolocating in the vicinity of a net, but concentrating on something else, such as a fish or another porpoise.

The total number of porpoises killed each year in fishing gear is unknown. What we do know is sobering. Every species, even the spectacled porpoise, is killed in commercial fisheries. Tens of thousands of harbor porpoises are killed in gill net fisheries each year throughout the northern hemisphere. Many thousands of Dall's porpoises have been taken over the past two decades in surface gill net fisheries in the North Pacific. In the past, several hundred Burmeister's porpoises were killed annually in gill nets along the coast of Peru, where their meat was sometimes used for human consumption. The finless porpoise inhabits some of most intensively fished areas of the world and, although we don't have estimates of the total number of animals killed each year, there is growing concern over the impact of fisheries on this species. The most dire situation involves the tiny and highly endangered vaquita, now reduced to a few hundred animals in the Gulf of California through accidental deaths in gill nets, and are still killed in fisheries there.

A few examples will illustrate the nature and magnitude of this problem. From surveys of the Gulf of California conducted by Mexican and American biologists, we know that the vaquita is restricted to a tiny portion of the northwestern Gulf. Perhaps 500 vaquitas remain in this area, which is fished intensively by a large number of Mexican fishermen. In the past, many vaquitas were killed in a gill net fishery for totoaba, a large sea bass, but this fishery has been closed to protect both the overfished totoaba and the endangered vaquita. Unfortunately, fishermen continue to use gill nets to catch a variety of other species of fish and shrimp; these nets also

Two porpoises in a herring weir awaiting release. Fatalities
are unusual, because porpoises can swim, breathe and feed in the weirs.
In most other cases, encounters between porpoises and fishing gear are fatal.

kill vaquitas. Working with the fishermen of El Golfo de Santa Clara – a small village in the Upper Gulf of California – conservation biologist Caterina D'Agrosa documented the deaths of 15 vaquitas in a little over a year. El Golfo de Santa Clara is only one of several ports in the fishing area, so this represents only a fraction of the total number of vaquitas killed each year. These deaths place the vaquita in imminent danger of extinction.

In the Gulf of Maine, fishermen set gill nets for cod and other bottom-dwelling species. These nets also catch large numbers of harbor porpoises. The US government estimates that the total number of porpoises killed in the Gulf of Maine and adjacent waters each year is in the range of 2100 to 2350. These deaths come from a population that is believed to contain about 45,000 individuals. Thus, although gill nets do not threaten the harbor porpoise population

A vaquita and her calf in the Gulf of California, Mexico.

with immediate extinction, as is the case with the vaquita, they kill more porpoises each year than are replaced through births. Over time, therefore, the population will slowly dwindle in size. Recognizing this situation, the US government has proposed that the harbor porpoise population of the Gulf of Maine should be added to the official list of species threatened with extinction. The problem is complicated by the fact that porpoises are killed in gill nets in both Canada and the United States. From our work in the Bay of Fundy, we know that porpoises move back and forth across the international boundary

The vaquita is the most endangered marine cetacean and only a few hundred remain in existence. Many vaquitas have been killed in gill net fisheries for species such as the totoaba, a large sea bass pictured here. Overfishing has also threatened the totoaba and other species in the northwestern Gulf of California. Immediate conservation measures are required to save the vaquita and totoaba from extinction.

into the Gulf of Maine and are vulnerable to gill nets on both sides of the border.

A similar situation exists in the North Sea, where harbor porpoises are killed in gill nets set by fishermen from many European countries. The best studied fleet is the Danish gill net fishery for cod, which kills more than 4500 porpoises annually. This one fishery takes approximately 2 per cent of the harbor porpoise population in the North Sea each year. The total number of porpoises killed in the North Sea by all fisheries is unknown.

A vaquita which perished in a gill net.

What can be done to reduce the numbers of porpoises killed in fishing nets each year? Current conservation efforts focus on two possible solutions. First, if it is possible to identify times and areas where large numbers of porpoises are killed, gill net fishing can be restricted from those areas. This requires accurate information on the numbers of porpoises killed in different areas and seasons.

Fortunately, many countries now place observers aboard fishing vessels to collect this type of information. In the Gulf of Maine, for example, most of the porpoises are caught on one particular fishing ground, known as Jeffreys Ledge. Closing this area to gill nets would greatly reduce the total number of porpoises killed by the fishery. This is obviously an attractive approach to conservation groups and many scientists, but it is widely opposed by fishermen,

Thousands of Dall's porpoises have been killed in commercial fisheries.

who do not want to be excluded from their favorite fishing grounds. Nevertheless, such fishery closures have been used as part of the strategy to reduce the number of porpoises killed by gill net fisheries in the Gulf of Maine and are being considered elsewhere. A similar approach may be needed in the Upper Gulf of California, where the Government of Mexico recently declared a Biosphere Reserve, in part to protect the totoaba and vaquita.

Second, many scientists and fishermen are experimenting with ways of making gill nets more detectable to porpoises. One of the most promising avenues of research is the development of acoustic alarms, placed on nets to warn porpoises of their presence. These alarms, also known as 'pingers', were first developed by psychologist Jon Lien to help prevent humpback whales from becoming entangled in cod traps off Newfoundland. Pingers produce a high-frequency sound that can be heard by whales, dolphins and porpoises, but not by cod. Gill net fishermen in the Gulf of Maine learned of Lien's work and decided to test pingers in their fishery. Many scientists, myself included, were skeptical of this idea, but a carefully designed experiment conducted on Jeffreys Ledge in 1994 showed that pingers could reduce the number of porpoises killed in gill nets by up to 90 per cent. Since that time, similar experiments have been conducted in the United States, Canada, and Scandinavia, with generally positive results.

We do not yet understand why pingers are effective. Porpoises may find their sound unpleasant and avoid a net equipped with the devices. It is also possible that porpoises do not find the sound aversive, but are alerted to the presence of a net by their sound, much as we respond to a flashing warning light on a street corner. It is less likely, but still possible, that pingers are effective because their prey do not like the sound they produce. Recent experiments have demonstrated that herring have an unusual capacity to hear the high frequency sound emitted by pingers. Some scientists have suggested that porpoises are less likely to be entangled in fishing nets equipped with pingers because herring will stay away from the devices. Experiments are being conducted to determine which of these mechanisms are responsible for the success of pingers in field trials.

Current evidence indicates that pingers may be effective in reducing the number of porpoises killed in gill net fisheries, but there are still many questions regarding their use. Some of the most pressing questions include: Who should pay for the alarms? Will they have adverse effects on other marine animals? Will porpoises habituate to them over time, making them less effective? And, finally, will fishermen use them properly, outside the controlled setting of an experiment? At the moment, we do not know the answers to these questions. It is clear, however, that careful testing and sober evaluation are necessary before pingers are accepted as the solution to by-catches of porpoises in gill nets.

Where populations of porpoises are under threat there is widespread agreement that the number of those killed should be reduced to insignificant levels or eliminated altogether. In other situations, there is no consensus whether or not the numbers of porpoises killed in a fishery should be reduced. I argue that, whether or not such by-catches are sustainable, the death of any porpoises in fishing gear is unnecessary and we should all work to eliminate such wasteful fishing practices. This is one goal that fishermen, scientists and conservationists should all agree on. Unfortunately, bringing about such change is very difficult. The entanglement of a small porpoise in a gill net does not cost a fisherman much time or money, so he is unlikely to change unless required to do so. Somehow, the cost of catching a porpoise, or the reward for not catching one, needs to be changed so that it makes economic sense for fishermen to change their practices. This is one area where market forces could play an important role: if the public were to demand that cod was captured in an environmentally sound fashion, fishermen might make more effort to eliminate by-catches of porpoises in their nets.

The conservation of porpoises requires collaboration among scientists, fishermen
and policy makers and support from the public. Innovative measures must be developed
to allow commercial fisheries and marine mammals, like these harbor porpoises, to co-exist.

Dall's porpoises are threatened by accidental mortality in commercial fisheries and from over-harvest in Japanese waters. Recent conservation measures have reduced the number of Dall's porpoises killed each year.

Porpoises also face a variety of other threats from human activities. They have been hunted for food and oil for centuries in several parts of the world. Their tissues are contaminated by pesticides and heavy metals. And they have been driven from parts of their habitat by coastal development, noise and disturbance.

Both Dall's and harbor porpoises have been hunted intensively over the past century. Large numbers of Dall's porpoises are still taken by harpoon in the coastal waters of Japan. The demand for porpoise meat increased dramatically in Japan after the moratorium on commercial whaling took effect and in 1988, over 40,000 Dall's porpoises were harpooned. The level of this directed hunting, which continues today, together with by-catches in commercial fisheries, has led to much concern over the status of Dall's porpoises in Japanese waters.

Harbor porpoises have been hunted in the Pacific, Atlantic, Baltic and Black Seas. The longest-standing hunt took place in the Danish straits that link the Baltic and Kattegat Seas. This hunt originated in the Stone Age and continued almost uninterrupted until the Second World War. The number of porpoises taken each year varied from the low hundreds to over 2000. The porpoises were driven into shallow coves, surrounded by nets and dragged ashore to be killed for meat and oil. Harbor porpoises have been hunted in many other areas, but the Danish hunt is one of the few to have its origins before the advent of firearms. In most other areas, it was not possible to catch harbor porpoises because they do not approach boats. Only the unusual topography of the Danish straits enabled the hunters there to drive porpoises ashore.

Many porpoises carry high levels of chemical pollutants in their tissues. This is particularly true of harbor porpoises, which often inhabit highly contaminated waters. Researchers have compiled a long list of the pollutants present in harbor porpoise tissues and documented levels of these contaminants in porpoises from different areas. This list includes organochlorines, such as DDT and PCBs, that accumulate in blubber, and heavy metals, such as mercury and cadmium, in other tissues. Unfortunately, we know very little about the effects of these pollutants on the health of porpoises. Pathologists have not documented evidence of acute effects of these chemicals, but what, if any, chronic effects they might have is unknown. Levels of DDT and PCBs have declined since their use was restricted, but in many areas levels in porpoise tissues are still high enough to warrant concern. Until more research is conducted to determine exactly what effects these contaminants have on porpoises and other marine mammals, we can only state a general concern over their presence in such high levels.

Finally, coastal porpoises must share their habitat with an ever-expanding human population. Noise pollution is an increasing problem in many areas. Even in the relatively pristine waters of the Bay of Fundy, noise is a growing threat to harbor porpoises. In an attempt to keep seals away from their cages, salmon farmers have resorted to using high intensity sound produced by 'seal scrammers'. Experiments conducted in British Columbia, and recently duplicated in the Bay of Fundy, indicate that these devices exclude porpoises from areas that are several miles in diameter. This noise, together with the increased boat traffic and habitat degradation associated with salmon farming, is reducing porpoise habitat in many areas of the Bay of Fundy and elsewhere where salmon farming is practiced. Perhaps the species most affected by human alteration of coastal habitat is the finless porpoise, which lives in the densely inhabited coastal areas of southeastern Asia. Although few scientific studies have been conducted on the effects of human activities on this species, there are many disturbing accounts of finless porpoises disappearing from large portions of their range.

Harbor porpoises are shy animals and sensitive to disturbance.

Towards the Future

Despite the litany of problems faced by porpoises, the news is not all bleak. There are a growing number of positive signs that we are making advances towards the conservation of porpoises. Public education campaigns by conservation and animal welfare groups are focused more and more frequently on porpoises, particularly on the harbor porpoise. In part, these campaigns are fueled by the findings of a growing number of researchers studying porpoises and conservation issues in North and South America, Europe and Asia.

Together, these efforts have led to some important advances. On a local scale, unlikely coalitions of individual scientists, fishermen and representatives from conservation groups have made considerable progress towards porpoise conservation. A good example of this type of collaboration was the 1994 experiment to test acoustic alarms on Jeffreys Ledge. Despite some initial mistrust on all sides, all parties worked together to provide the best test possible of these devices. Fishermen learned about the design of scientific experiments, scientists gained a new respect for the hazards of working at sea, and the experiment could never have occurred without political pressure from conservation groups. The positive outcome of the experiment provided a new tool with which to reduce the number of porpoises killed in gill nets.

Other conservation victories have been made within the context of national legislation. In Peru, for example, Burmeister's porpoises and several species of dolphins have been killed deliberately for their meat. Biologists Koen Van Waerebeek and Julio Reyes, working with very little financial or political support, lobbied successfully for passage of a law protecting all dolphins and porpoises from intentional harm. At first the law was ineffective, as animals

An aerial view of two porpoises at the surface.

continued to be killed and their meat sold illegally on the black market. Undeterred, Julio and Koen conducted a tireless education and media campaign and have since greatly reduced the number of animals killed in this manner. Perhaps more importantly, they have changed the attitude of a generation of young Peruvians towards these animals.

There have also been success stories at the international level. One of the most promising signs of progress was the signing of the Agreement on Small Cetaceans of the Baltic and North Seas (ASCOBANS) by many northern European countries. This important agreement provides harbor porpoises with some level of protection from a variety of human activities. The countries that are party to this agreement agreed to work towards reducing by-catches in fisheries, preventing the release of potentially harmful toxic substances, protecting food resources and preventing disturbance.

Many challenges lie ahead, particularly in finding methods to reduce the number of porpoises killed in commercial fisheries. Scientists need to work towards understanding why porpoises become entangled in fishing nets. Fishermen need to develop cleaner and more efficient fishing methods that do not cause the deaths of so many porpoises. Policy makers need to develop and implement effective conservation measures to protect these animals. Ultimately, however, none of this will happen unless there is a public demand for such action. What can you do? Join a conservation or animal welfare organization that is concerned about the plight of these animals. Find out where your seafood comes from and how it is caught. And ask your politicians about their support for environmental legislation.

In the Bay of Fundy we often take our boat out to an area where porpoises congregate to feed in a tide rip. If we shut the motor off and drift, porpoises sometimes swim by and glance up at us. Occasionally, one of those porpoises is wearing a plastic fin tag, indicating that we released it from a herring weir. These encounters are a good reminder of why the hard work is worth it.

A gray Dall's porpoise in Washington State, U.S.A.
This animal has facial features of both Dall's porpoises and
harbor porpoises and may represent a hybrid between the two species.

Porpoises live in coastal waters, where human activities are most
keenly felt. Even in Alaska, where these Dall's porpoises are found, humans
have altered and degraded coastal ecosystems. The disappearance of porpoises from
many coastal areas should serve as a reminder of their vulnerability and of the fragile nature
of their habitat. We have a responsibility to ensure the survival of these animals and their world.

(Top) A harbor porpoise surfaces in the Bay of Fundy.
(Bottom) Dall's porpoises bow-riding in the North Pacific.

Porpoise Facts

Common Name: Harbor Porpoise
Scientific Name: *Phocoena phocoena*
Maximum Length: 6 ft 6 in (2 m)
Distribution: Coastal Northern Hemisphere

Common Name: Burmeister's Porpoise
Scientific Name: *Phocoena spinipinnis*
Maximum Length: 6 ft 6 in (2 m)
Distribution: Coastal South America

Common Name: Vaquita
Scientific Name: *Phocoena sinus*
Maximum Length: 4 ft 11 in (1.5 m)
Distribution: Coastal Gulf of California

Common Name: Finless Porpoise
Scientific Name: *Neophocaena phocaenoides*
Maximum Length: 6 ft 2 in (1.9 m)
Distribution: Coastal Southern and Eastern Asia

Common Name: Dall's Porpoise
Scientific Name: *Phocoenoides dalli*
Maximum Length: 7 ft 2 in (2.2 m)
Distribution: North Pacific

Common Name: Spectacled Porpoise
Scientific Name: *Australophocoena dioptrica*
Maximum Length: 7 ft 2 in (2.2 m)
Distribution: Offshore Subantarctic

Biographical Note

Andrew Read is an assistant professor in the Nicholas School of the Environment, Duke University. He teaches and studies the ecology and conservation biology of marine mammals at the Duke University Marine Laboratory. He has been studying porpoises since 1980, conducting field work in North America, South America and Europe. Andy lives in Beaufort, North Carolina, with his wife Kim and two cats.

Index

*Entries in **bold** indicate pictures*

Recommended Reading

Biology of the Phocoenids, edited by Arne Bjorge and Greg Donovan and published in 1995 as *Special Issue 16 of the Reports of the International Whaling Commission* in Cambridge, UK. A compendium of scientific papers on the biology and conservation of porpoises.

The Sierra Club Handbook of Whales and Dolphins, by Stephen Leatherwood and Randall Reeves, published by Sierra Club Books, San Francisco, in 1983. Far and away the best field guide to dolphins, porpoises and whales.

The Ecology of Whales and Dolphins, by David Gaskin, published by Heinemann Educational Books, London, in 1982. A comprehensive account of the ecology of cetaceans, written by an expert on harbor porpoises.

Whales, by E.J. Slijper, published by Hutchinson and Company, London, in 1962. A classic, and although slightly dated, still the definitive account of the general biology of cetaceans, with many insights into the biology of harbor porpoises.